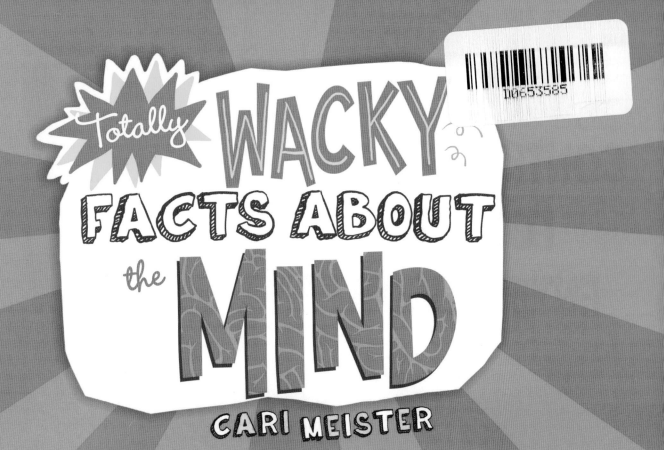

Totally WACKY FACTS ABOUT the MIND

CARI MEISTER

raintree

a Capstone company — publishers for children

THE BRAIN IS LIKE THE CONTROL ROOM FOR THE ENTIRE BODY.

YOU CAN'T DANCE WITHOUT YOUR BRAIN.

No one understands exactly how the mind works.

YOU CAN'T EVEN BREATHE WITHOUT YOUR BRAIN!

A BABY'S SKULL IS PARTLY OPEN TO MAKE ROOM FOR ITS BRAIN TO GROW.

A baby's brain doubles in size in the first year.

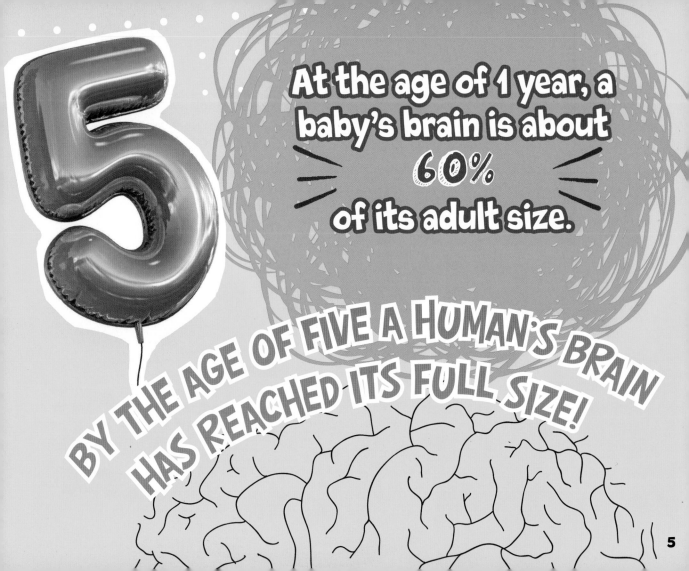

5

At the age of 1 year, a baby's brain is about **60%** of its adult size.

BY THE AGE OF FIVE A HUMAN'S BRAIN HAS REACHED ITS FULL SIZE!

LEARNING NEW THINGS HELPS YOUR BRAIN TO GROW.

A 3-YEAR-OLD'S BRAIN IS 2½ TIMES MORE ACTIVE THAN AN ADULT'S BRAIN.

ONE STUDY SAYS THAT THE BRAINS OF MEN AND WOMEN ARE WIRED DIFFERENTLY.

Women and men use different brain parts to do the same activities.

THE AVERAGE BRAIN WEIGHS ABOUT 1.3 KILOGRAMS (3 POUNDS) AND IS THE SIZE OF A CANTALOUPE MELON.

ON AVERAGE, **MEN HAVE** BIGGER **BRAINS THAN WOMEN.**

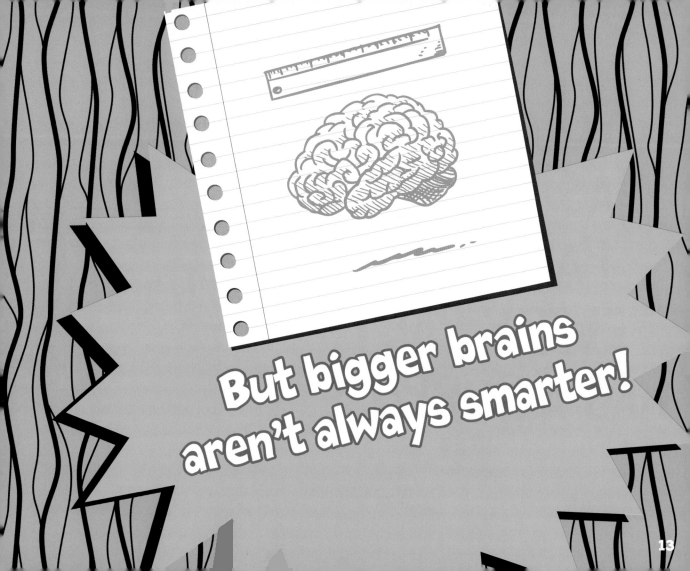

But bigger brains aren't always smarter!

YOUR BRAIN HAS FIVE MAIN PARTS, AND EVERY PART HAS A PURPOSE.

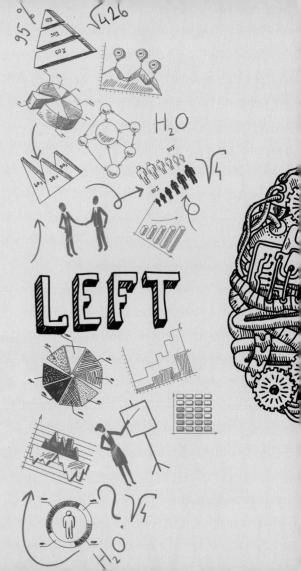

Right

EACH SIDE OF YOUR BRAIN CONTROLS THE OPPOSITE SIDE OF YOUR BODY.

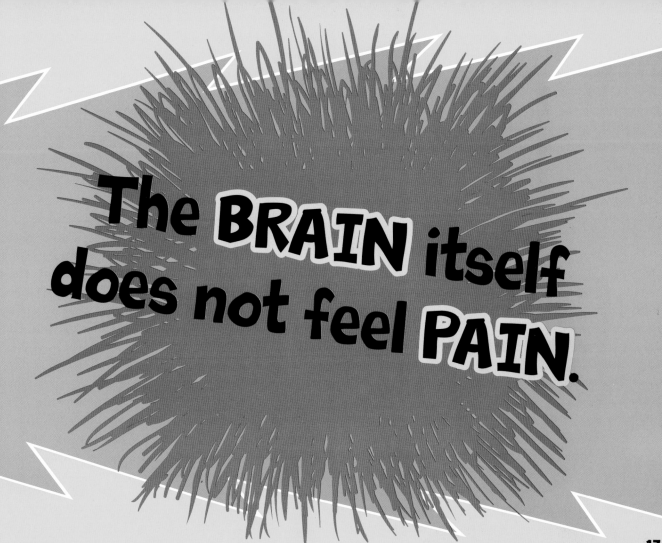

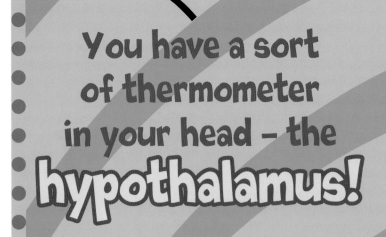

You have a sort
of thermometer
in your head – the
hypothalamus!

THIS PEARL-SIZED PART OF THE BRAIN CONTROLS YOUR TEMPERATURE.

A BRAIN PART CALLED THE AMYGDALA HELPS YOU TO READ OTHER PEOPLE'S EMOTIONS.

It's also the part that tells you to SCREAM when you're scared!

21

Like monarch butterflies, humans may have an internal compass.

CAN WE TRAVEL AROUND THE WORLD WITHOUT HELP FROM A COMPASS?

YOUR BRAIN FEELS
A BIT SLIMY,
LIKE JELLY.

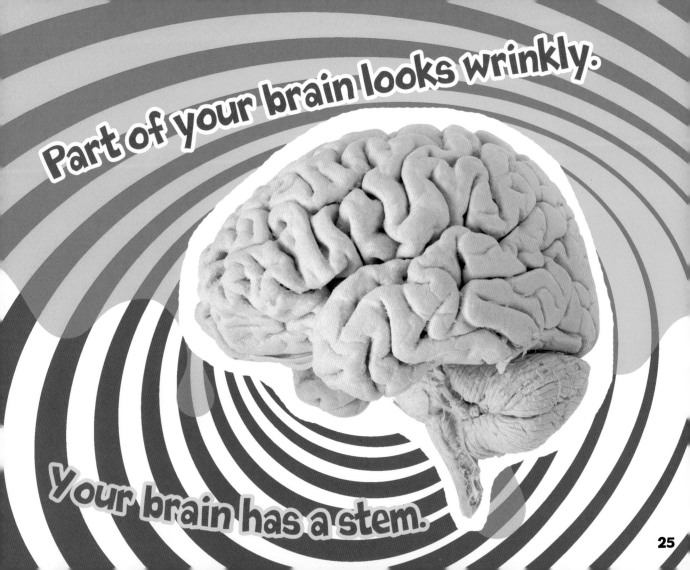

Part of your brain looks wrinkly.

Your brain has a stem.

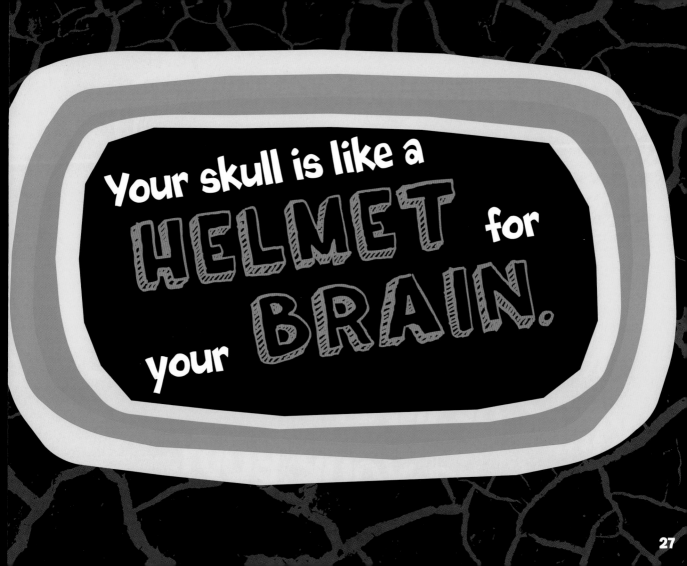

Your skull is like a HELMET for your BRAIN.

There are about 86 billion neurons in your brain.

NEURONS TRANSMIT ALL KINDS OF INFORMATION ALL OVER YOUR BODY.

It would take you more than three years to count all your neurons!

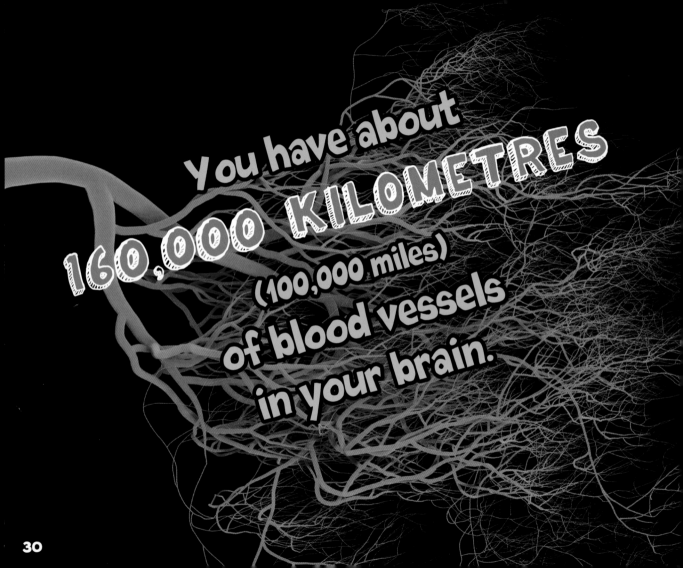

You have about 160,000 KILOMETRES (100,000 miles) of blood vessels in your brain.

EVERY MINUTE ABOUT THREE DRINK CANS WORTH OF BLOOD FLOWS TO THE BRAIN.

YOUR BRAIN MAKES ENOUGH ENERGY TO POWER A LIGHT BULB.

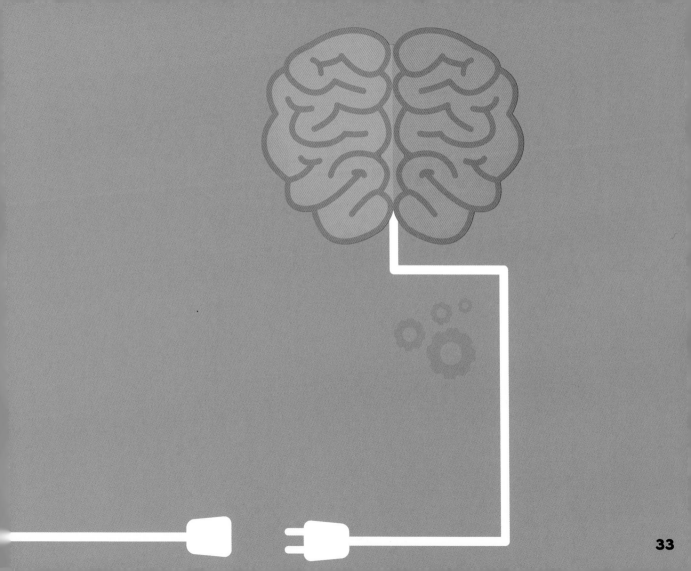

The outside of your brain is pink.

Parts of the brain are white.

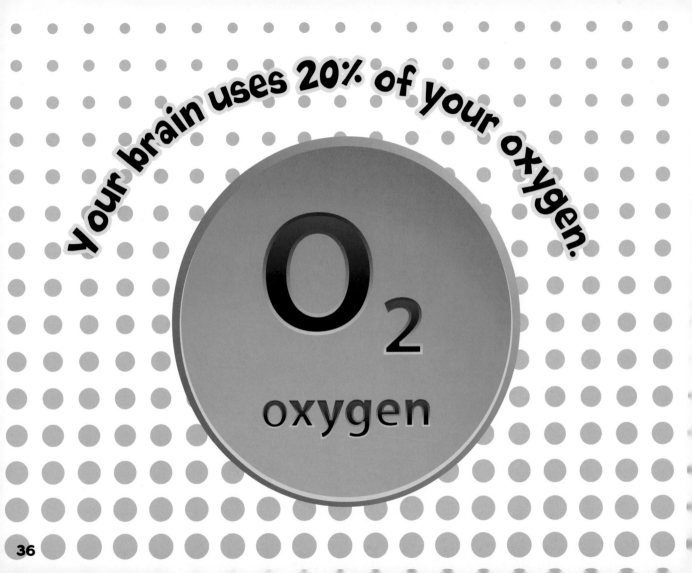

Your brain uses 20% of your oxygen.

O_2

oxygen

4 TO 6 MINUTES: THE AMOUNT OF TIME YOUR BRAIN CAN LIVE WITHOUT OXYGEN

THE UNITED STATES HAS PERFORMED MORE LOBOTOMIES THAN ANY OTHER COUNTRY.

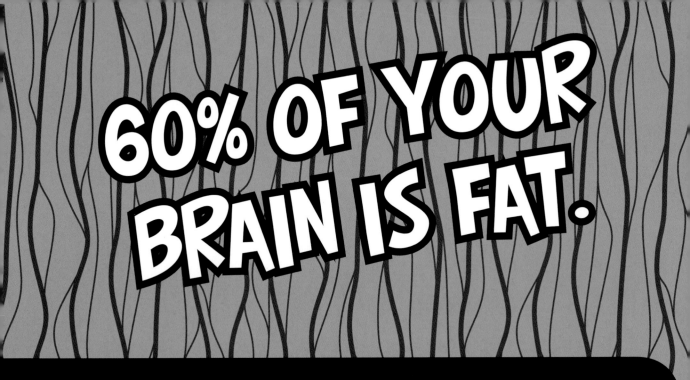

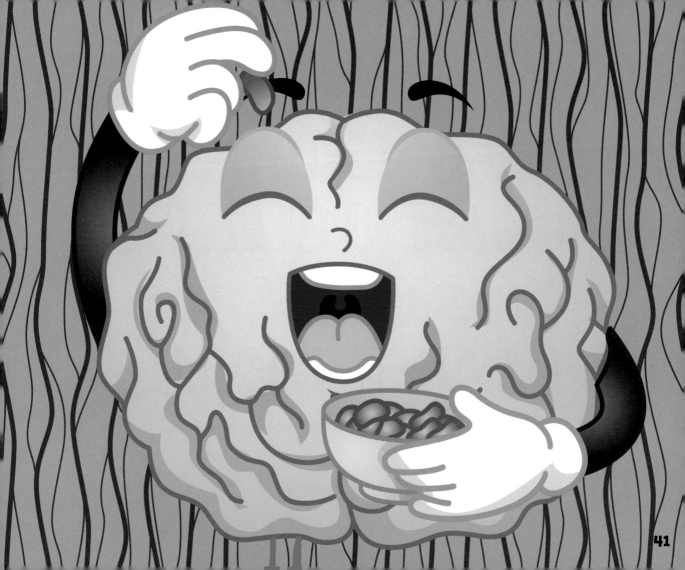

IT'S A MYTH THAT HUMANS USE ONLY 10% OF THE BRAIN.

Throughout a single day, we actually use all parts of the brain.

BRAINS HAVE NOT YET BEEN TRANSPLANTED, BUT ONE DAY THEY COULD BE!

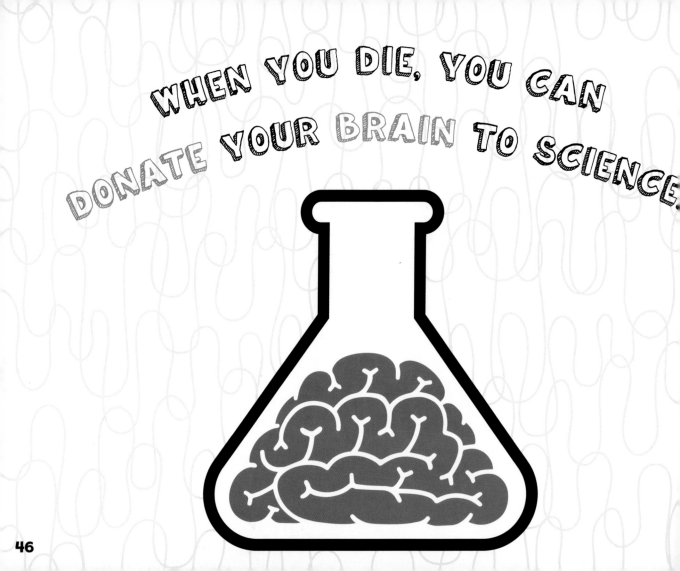

WHEN YOU DIE, YOU CAN DONATE YOUR BRAIN TO SCIENCE.

46

HARVARD UNIVERSITY IN THE UNITED STATES KEEPS A BRAIN BANK OF ABOUT 3,000 BRAINS.

Your brain can process information very quickly - about 430 kilometres (268 miles) per hour.

Your body can sense **11 MILLION** bits of information per second.

You can process only about **40** of these pieces of information.

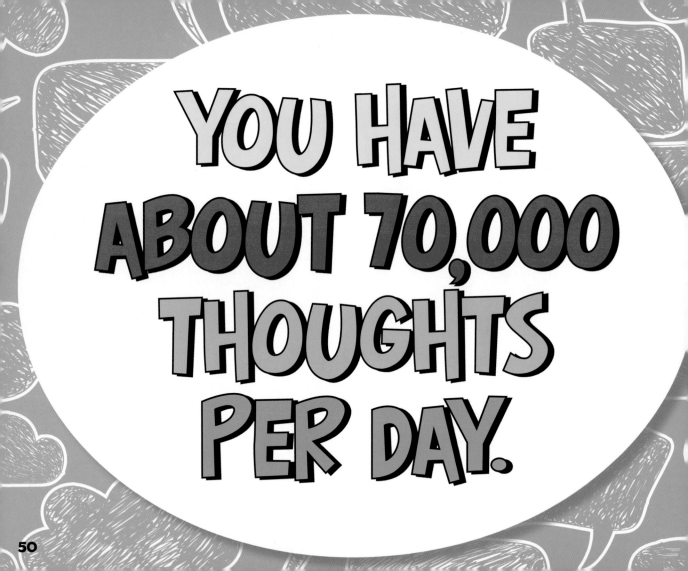

DAYDREAMING IS GOOD FOR YOUR MIND.

The average person daydreams about 47 per cent of the day.

Daydreaming helps your brain to make new connections.

A PHYSICAL PATH IS MADE IN YOUR BRAIN WHENEVER YOU HAVE A THOUGHT.

The more times you have had a thought, the easier it is to have again.

THINK GOOD THOUGHTS! IT WILL MAKE YOU A HAPPIER PERSON.

Only about **10%** of the population is left-handed.

MICHELANGELO AND DA VINCI WERE LEFT-HANDED

ONE STUDY CLAIMS THAT LEFT-HANDED PEOPLE DO BETTER ON IMPORTANT TESTS.

It also claims that left-handed people get scared more easily than those who are right-handed.

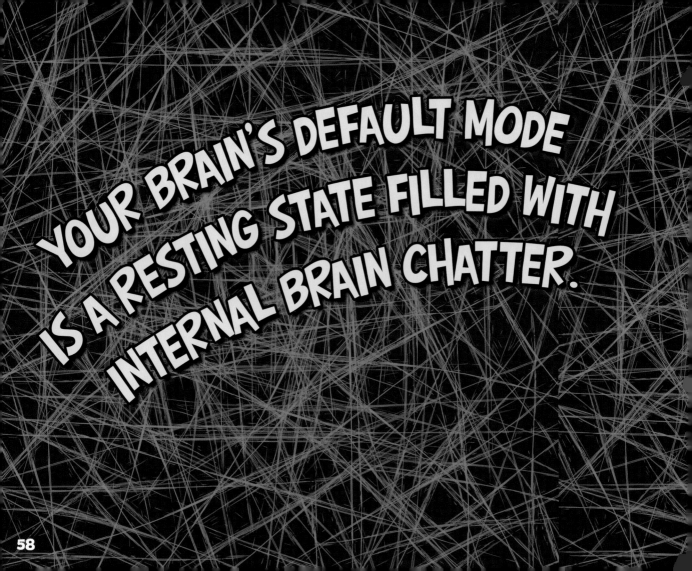

YOUR BRAIN'S DEFAULT MODE IS A RESTING STATE FILLED WITH INTERNAL BRAIN CHATTER.

In this resting state, your brain uses a lot of energy!

Things we see all the time can be easily forgotten because we see them so often.

Your brain changes your memories when you talk about them.

SOME PEOPLE BELIEVE THEIR MINDS CAN PREDICT THE FUTURE. THEY CALL THEMSELVES CLAIRVOYANTS.

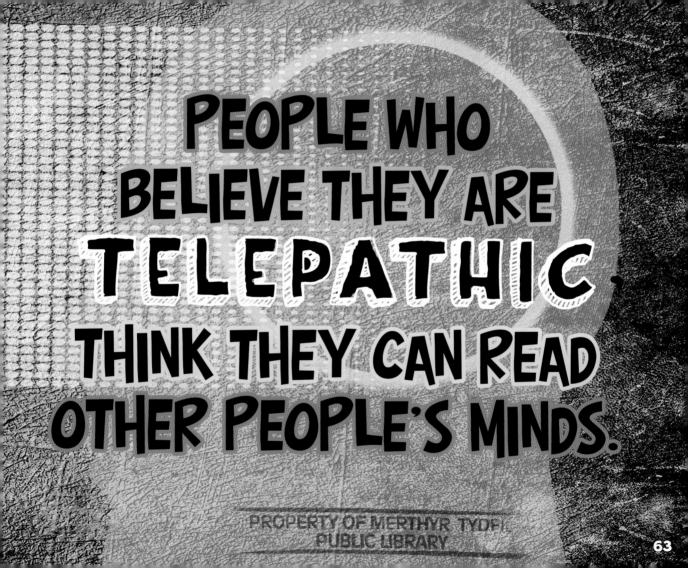

PEOPLE WHO BELIEVE THEY ARE **TELEPATHIC**, THINK THEY CAN READ OTHER PEOPLE'S MINDS.

ESP stands for "extra sensory perception".

PEOPLE WHO THINK THEY HAVE ESP BELIEVE THEY CAN SENSE THINGS WITH THEIR MINDS.

Déjà vu is like a brain hiccup. It happens when there is a brain malfunction.

SOME PEOPLE BELIEVE DÉJÀ VU HAPPENS WHEN TWO UNIVERSES COLLIDE.

DÉJÀ VU IS FRENCH FOR "ALREADY SEEN".

Jigsaw puzzles

exercise parts of the brain.

THERE IS NO SUCH THING AS A TRULY PHOTOGRAPHIC MEMORY.

Some people can memorize
the order of a pack of cards
in under one minute.

COLOURS CAN INSPIRE OUR BRAINS TO THINK IN A CERTAIN WAY.

The colour blue sparks CREATIVITY.

The colour green makes people feel relaxed.

A TEENAGER NEEDS 9¼ HOURS OF SLEEP FOR HIS BRAIN TO FUNCTION PROPERLY.

If you get a good night's sleep, you will be able to concentrate better.

MOST TEENAGERS DON'T GET ENOUGH SLEEP.

Some people say you can't DREAM and SNORE at the same time.

NUMBER OF DREAMS IN A LIFETIME:

100,000

EVERYONE DREAMS. YOU JUST FORGET MOST OF YOUR DREAMS.

People who are blind dream.

A BLIND PERSON'S BRAIN IS ABLE TO REWIRE ITSELF, GIVING HER A HEIGHTENED SENSE OF HEARING.

REAL LAUGHTER HAPPENS UNCONSCIOUSLY.

Laughter activates five different parts of the brain.

IN CREATIVE THINKING, THERE IS NEVER ONE ANSWER.

To be creative, you must practise being creative.

A recent study found that there is a network over a large area of the brain that is used during creative thinking.

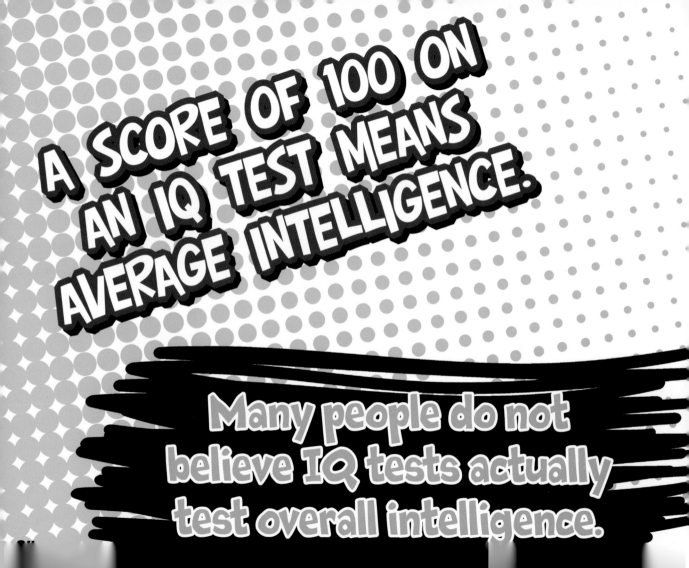

HIGHEST ADULT IQ ON RECORD: 198

MUSIC CAN HEAL THE BRAIN.

MUSIC HELPS PEOPLE FEEL POSITIVE.

MUSIC CAN REDUCE PAIN.

Music can transport your mind back in time.

Musical training helps some children improve their reading.

KNITTING IS GOOD FOR YOUR BRAIN. IT REDUCES STRESS AND ANXIETY.

LIKE PUZZLES, BRAIN GAMES HELP TO IMPROVE YOUR ABILITY TO REASON.

OPTICAL ILLUSIONS TRICK THE BRAIN.

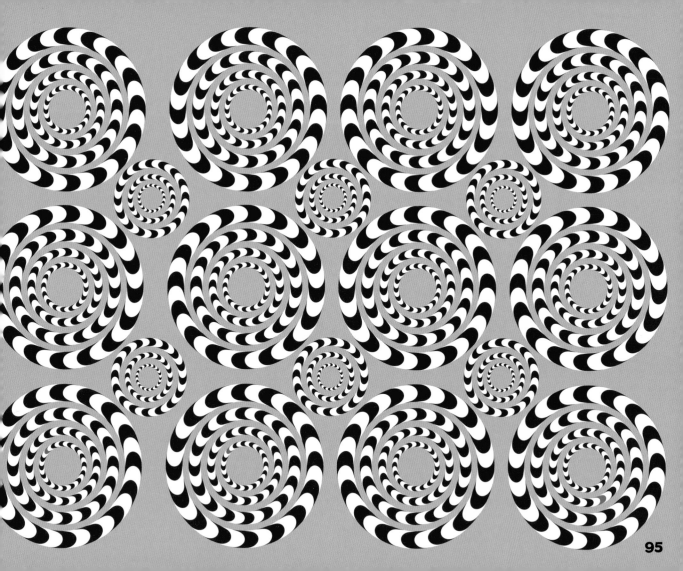

Reading to children makes them smarter.

If you read for 20 minutes a day, you will be exposed to around 1.8 million words a year!

People who read for fun usually do better at school.

When you see someone hit his head, the same pain area in your brain lights up.

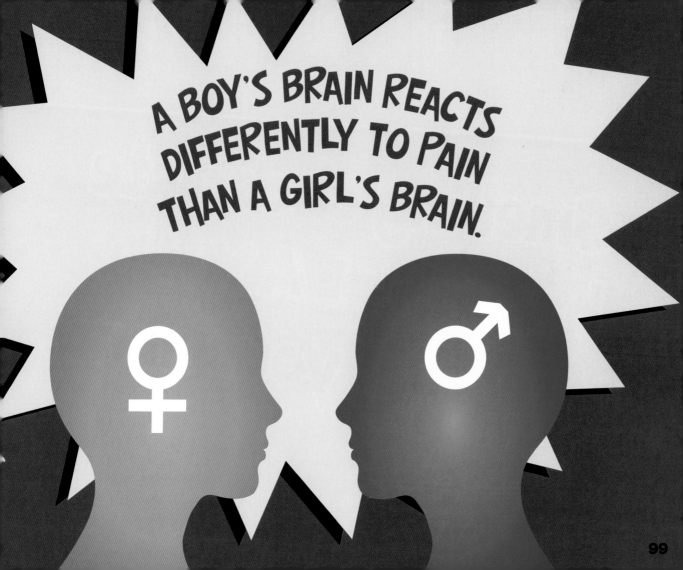

Smelling chocolate has a RELAXING effect on your mind.

EATING CHOCOLATE SENDS A RUSH OF BLOOD TO AREAS OF YOUR BRAIN.

ONE THEORY CLAIMS THAT EATING FOODS WITH ARTIFICIAL COLOURS SLOWS DOWN YOUR THINKING.

Highly processed foods trick your brain into wanting more.

EATING FISH CAN HELP TO KEEP YOUR BRAIN HEALTHY.

The best foods for your brain: blueberries, avocados, nuts and seeds

ABOUT 90% OF SICKNESS AND DISEASE IS RELATED TO STRESS IN YOUR MIND.

BEING PHYSICALLY FIT HELPS YOUR BRAIN TO STAY HEALTHY.

You think more clearly after exercising.

Ways to boost your brainpower:

EXERCISE EVERY DAY

SLEEP WELL

KEEP LEARNING

GLOSSARY

amygdala small groups of cells in your brain that are responsible for your feelings

anxiety feeling of worry or fear

hypothalamus part of your brain that regulates your body temperature

IQ intelligence quotient; a number used to measure someone's intelligence

lobotomy surgical operation on the brain

mature having reached full growth or development

neuron nerve cell

optical illusion something that makes us see things that do not exist or are different from how they appear

photographic memory memory that is capable of retaining information that is as clear as a photograph

process put through a series of tasks

theory idea that explains something that is unknown

transplant remove and replace

READ MORE

The Human Body (Essential Life Science), Melanie Waldron (Raintree, 2013)

Sight (The Science Behind), Louise Spilsbury (Raintree, 2012)

Utterly Amazing Human Body, Robert Winston (DK Children, 2015)

Your Brain: Understand it with numbers (Your Body By Numbers), Melanie Waldron (Raintree, 2014)

WEBSITES

www.bbc.co.uk/scotland/brainsmart/brain/

Learn more about your brain, including ti[p]
to keep it healthy!

www.dkfindout.com/uk/human-body/brain-and-nerves/

Discover more about your brain and nerv[ous]
system.

INDEX

Raintree is an imprint of Capstone Global Library Limited, a company incorporated in England and Wales having its registered office at 264 Banbury Road, Oxford, OX2 7DY – Registered company number: 6695582

www.raintree.co.uk
myorders@raintree.co.uk

Editor: Shelly Lyons
Designer: Lori Bye
Media Researcher: Jo Miller

ISBN 978 1 4747 1279 8
20 19 18 17 16
10 9 8 7 6 5 4 3 2 1

British Library Cataloguing in Publication Data
A full catalogue record for this book is available from the British Library.

Acknowledgements
We would like to thank the following for permission to reproduce photographs: Dreamstime: Akulamatiau, Cover (bottom right), 51; Shutterstock: Aaron Amat, 37, aboikis, Cover (top right), advent, 13, Africa Studio, 24, Aleksandr Khakimullin, 75, Alexilus, Cover (bottom left), Andrei Tarchyshnik, 86, Aniwhite, 79, Anna Shkolnaya, 50-51, Bard Sandemose, 57, Blend Images, 11, Cloud7Days, 10-11, Complot, 44, Cory Thoman, 61, Dan Kosmayer, 31, Daxiao Productions, 2, Deborah Kolb, 43, DenisFilm, 89, Dooder, 85, Fabio Berti, 38, Flegere, 8-9, Gala, 72, Gelpi JM, 4, glenda, 25, Halfpoint, 7, Halfpoint, 82-83, Hardyguardy, 20-21 (top and bottom), Igor Zh., 42-43, Incomible, 64-65, Ivelin Radkov, 90-91, Iveta Angelova, 67, Johavel, 76, jps, 22, kasahasa, 32-33, Konstantin Inozemtsev, 30, Kostiantyn Fastov, 105, koya979, 5, lanych, 12, Ljupco Smokovski, 104, Ljupco Smokovski, 108, lolloj, 62-63, LongQuattro, 36, Lorelyn Medina, 41, lotan, 95, Lyudmyla Kharlamova, 70-71, Macrovector, 14-15, Madlen, 102, Marco Govel, 101, Maridav, 106, Marie Maerz, 91, matimix, 107, Matthias G. Ziegler, 87, Monkik, 47, Moofer, Cover (top left), Morphart Creation, 39, musicman, 65, Orhan Cam, 96, PathDoc, 52, Petr Vaclavek, 68-69, pio3, 99, Piotr Marcinski, 21, ra2studio, 55, ratch, 54, Roman Sigaev, 71, RONORMANJR, 3, Sam72, 16, Samuel Borges Photography, 109, Sanjacm, 56, Sergey Furtaev, 81, Sergey Shenderovsky, 59, Shirstok, 48, SoRad, 46, sumire8, 23, totallyPic.com, 92, Valery Sidelnykov, 9, Vector for u, 2-3, VIGE.CO, 18 (bottom), VitaminCo, 26, vitstudio, 28, vivat, 18 (top), Vladimir Matvienko, 58-59, wavebreakmedia, 60.

Design elements by Capstone and Shutterstock.

Every effort has been made to contact copyright holders of material reproduced in this book. Any omissions will be rectified in subsequent printings if notice is given to the publisher.

All the internet addresses (URLs) given in this book were valid at the time of going to press. However, due to the dynamic nature of the internet, some addresses may have changed, or sites may have changed or ceased to exist since publication. While the author and publisher regret any inconvenience this may cause readers, no responsibility for any such changes can be accepted by either the author or the publisher.

Printed and bound in China